More praise for Des Mannay

A great first collection by Mannay and I look forward to reading more from him.

Matt Duggan, editor of *The Angry Manifesto*,
winner *Into the Void* Prize 2016, *Erbacce Prize* 2015

Des Mannay goes some distance in dismantling power structures, abusers, criminals to the body and spirit: 'You are no longer/scary, all/powerful – I/am no longer/in your grasp.' Yes! to this.

Clare E Potter, winner of the *John Tripp Award*

Des Mannay gives voice to prejudices suffered in these crazy days.

Reuben Woolley, editor of *I Am Not A Silent Poet*

Des Mannay

Sod 'em – and tomorrow

First published in 2020
by Waterloo Press (Hove)
95 Wick Hall
Furze Hill
Hove BN3 1NG

Printed in Palatino 10pt by
One Digital
54 Hollingdean Road
East Sussex BN2 4AA

A CIP record for this book is available
from the British Library

ISBN: 978-1-906742-78-2

Acknowledgements

I'd like to gratefully acknowledge the award of a Creative Futures Gold award and mentorship in 2015, studying with Simon Jenner through the linked Mentorship programme at New Writing South.

I'd like to thank those involved in the awards of Rethinkyourmind Poetry Competiton 2015, Disability Arts Cymru Competition 2015 (2nd and Highly Commended Prizes).

In addition I'm grateful to the editors of the following journals and anthologies for permission to republish the following poems. The Angry Manifesto, Proletarian Poetry, and Onward/Ymlaen, 2020 Culture Matters - all for 'And the Dead Shall Rise'. The Angry Manifesto for 'Lieberries' and 'We Fought The Law Back'. Creative Futures Literary Awards 2015, and Hiraeth/Erzolirzoli: Wales - Cameroon anthology 2018 for 'They Call Me'. Hiraeth/Erzolirzoli: Wales - Cameroon anthology, Hafan 2018, Proletarian Poetry, and the Erbacce Journal for 'On the death of Muhammad Ali'. Hiraeth/Erzolirzoli: Wales - Cameroon anthology, Hafan 2018 for 'wallet'. International Times for 'Flood', 'paws for thought' and 'Shoes'. I Am Not A Silent Poet online journal, for 'The Blast', 'You're never alone with a loan', 'To a Lib-Dem Candidate' and 'You Never Arrived'. I Am Not A Silent Poet online journal and Moving Beyond Mars: a voice for victims/survivors of abuse Volume 1, 2018 Red Dashboard, USA, for 'Abuse Of Power'.

Allan o'r Golwg/Out of Sight by Disability Arts Cymru, 2018, for 'Barmpot'. Disability Arts Cymru inaugural poetry competition 2015, and the anthology Please hear what I'm not saying, Fly on the Wall Poetry 2018, for 'Recovery'. Disability Arts Cymru anthology 2016 for 'Is Not A Home....'. Poetry24 online journal and The Erbacce Journal for 'Peach', Poetry24 online journal for 'Lynch Mob', and 'Would That I'd Have Died That Night?'. Further Within Darkness and Light, Nothing Books, 2018 for 'Another Day' and 'That's Life'. MADDER THAN WE LOOK, Big White Shed 2016, for 'The Girl Who Jumped When Things Went Bang'.

The John Tripp and Idris Davies Poetry competition (2016) anthology for 'A Child's Purgatory In Wales'. How Well You Walk Through Madness; An Anthology of Beat, Weasel Press, USA, 2017 for 'Desolation'. Red Poets magazine for 'Homeless', 'Abandon', and 'Cladding'. No Tribal Dance anthology, Bristol 2017, and volume 1 of Persian Sugar in English Tea : a bilingual anthology of short poems and Haiku, New York/USA 2018, for 'Stoned'. Rhyme and Real Ale volume 2 - the next generation, Cardiff 2015, for 'The Remote Console'. The Round Up red light edition for 'What's love got to do with it?'. Stand Up And Spit for 'Ta Ta Tan Toc?'. The Scum Gentry Alternative Arts and Media, and The Erbacce Journal, for 'The ghost of Frida Kahlo'. Nuclear Impact: Broken Atoms in our Hands , 2017 Shabda Press USA, for 'My Last Journey'. The Erbacce Journal for 'Heads and Hearts'.

Contents

III.

I.

'Poets, by which I mean all artists, are finally the only people who know the truth about us. Soldiers don't. Statesmen don't. Priests don't. Union leaders don't. Only poets.'
James Baldwin

And The Dead Shall Rise

And what price did you pay for the silence?
The ultimate price: 266 men sent to the grave
in Gresford in 1934 – most still underground
The mine, the pit – not just the beating heart of Wales
but every mining community within its borders and beyond
made sclerotic by greedy coal owners,
who bought up Davy Lamps with the promise of safety,
but used them to place men in greater danger in pursuit of profit
Until the damps, the gases, suffocated you
You were betrayed – murdered – by your bosses,
now their spiritual great-grandchildren are coming for you
They want to desecrate your graves boys –
rip the poison gas from your lungs for profit
They may not have God on their side – but they have politicians and
    Court Orders
allowing them to pump chemicals and sand suspended in water
into the ground – shattering the shale, and your bodies too
Leaving your relatives to cope with yet another disaster
Like a Canary in a coal mine, environmental activists are there
warning of the impending danger brought on by a bunch of Frackers
When Bailiffs destroy their protest camp,
just like Canaries, they fly to another field and begin again
And colliery widows march down pneumoconiosis avenues
to offer support to the protesters
Because if they fail the dead shall rise
shattered into tiny fragments – along with the shale....

On the death of Muhammad Ali

Goodbye butterfly.
You stung like a bee.
You stung me!
From you I learnt
resistance!
To all the
'nigger, nigger – pull the trigger'
playground taunts
I could reply –
"C'mon Bugner!"

The kids at school
never listened
to 'Blue Mink'.
They didn't know
that what we
needed was
a great big melting pot.
My parents did –
they had me.

The 'Ugandan Asian' crisis hit
and I became
a 'Paki' overnight
because Enoch was right
and I should go back
to where I came from
even though
I was 'there' already.
And to some Asian kids
I was a 'gori'.

And the white girls
didn't stay too long
because they
didn't want to be
called "dogmeat!"
by their peers.
Shove thy neighbour.
So tell me –
what the hell
is the colour of love?

And the 'Rastas'
wore Wales football tops –
they were red
gold and green.
To them I was
a threat also –
'Babylon!'
I could not
go back to Africa;
a place I'd
never been.
And my heroes
all spoke perfect English –
Sidney Poitier, CLR James.

The old-old ladies
in Cardiff's docks
told me about
Africans –
when they came,
how tall they were,
how smart they were
in top hats, spats and canes...

And my grandad
was a 'Cru' man
and then he
joined a crew.
He sailed
and settled in
the bay of Tigers –
raised a family.
And my father was a 'half caste' -
that's what they
said back then.
And he would
sing Calypso
as he did
the washing up –
but said
Jamaicans were
johnny-come-lately's.
As I got older
boundaries blurred.
Bigotry
rescinded
like the tide,
I became
'exotic' –
Amerindian?
Latin-American?
Because of long
straight black hair
and Melanin
darkened skin –
myth-maken identity
yet again.

I don't know
where I come from –
but you don't know
where I'm going.
I worry the tide is
coming in again
and sometimes I
(really do) "feel like
throwing my hands
up in the air"
so – goodbye butterfly,
you have spread
your wings. And I
have been stung.

Lynch Mob
for Rashan Charles

CCTV footage
murder in
a corner shop
lynching dressed
up as
stop and search

What colour is
your hatred officer?
Black?
I see you and
fear for my sons

You used to
lynch in cells
now in our streets as well
we must claim
them back

Our anger is
the colour
of justice
resistance
our defence
No justice – no peace.

Flood

River of tears
salty wet
from giving birth
womb of winds
storm of floods
Texas, Louisiana –
death floats in streets

Buffoon flies in
for TV lens
photo opportunity
politicians only
talk in numbers,
$7.5 million –
auction begins

South East Asia
levee breaks
displacement figure
outbids cash of
American leaders
numbers crunch
like bullets fired
from a machine gun

Elsewhere in the
land of the free
corn crops rot as
vast underground lakes
aquifers, are bled dry
just caverns now

Without water
we cannot survive
with flood water
we cannot survive
Forget the oil wars –
the next 'great' war
will be for water

They Call Me

They call me Atticus
  'coz I live in an attic

They call me Platypus
  because I duck my bills

They call me often
  until they've had their fill

They call me sicknote
  because I'm often ill

They call me a cab
  but never pay the meter

They call me 'Mr Loverman'
  but hope I'll never meet her

They call me an alien
  though I'm not from outer space

They call me 'Johnnie foreigner'
  although I'm from this place

They call me wildcat
  when I go on strike

They sound like Norman Tebbit
  when they say, "On yer bike!"

They call me Ivan
  when I've an awful cough

They call me a dosser
  when I'm sleeping rough

All the things they call me
  won't catch me when I fall

I'd prefer they didn't
  call me anything at all

Just walking

Taking in the night air,
waiting for the nightmare.
Or will it be a dream?
Walking past the old factory,
which spews out its pollution.

      Along the river bank
      where dossers and tramps sleep.
      There is no natural route
      from brewery to drunk.
      Their own ruined lives –
      embers of a dying flame
      which once lit their bodies with life.
      The river carries the past to the present.

            The city holds a million untold stories
            locked behind closed doors
            which sometimes break out into the
            streets – liberated; all seen.

Journalists re-write them –
tabloid diamond sleazers –
into victims, or animals
which deserve no pity.
The type behind the typeface forgotten,
their lives carry on - like the river to the sea.

      Negotiating the Taff's rocks and whirlpools,
      cars drive through night-time's ghost roads.
      Hours ago the town would breathe out people,
      now darkness draws its breath and tucks them in.

A time to walk and clear the mind of
countless thoughts gathered through the day.
We live inside this prison –
invisible bars prevent us breaking free.
Only late night thoughts pass
easily between them.

Tear away the chains which bind my tongue
Unwrap the blindfold –
let me walk pavements of truth.

The distraught are not the vanquished,
or masters of their destiny.
We cannot clean the city streets
by scraping them till they shine with our skin.
The selfish cut to the bone for
the banquet of the unknown glutton

Surely there is a better way of living?
I know this is true –
the river told me so.

It carried the past to the present –
like the river to the sea.
I waited for the nightmare –
this time it will be a dream.

Peach

Plum.
Liked soccer –
quiet, intense teacher
trade unionist
socialist.

Overt stammer
explosive repetitions
facial tremor
sudden rush of words
so much to say
couldn't get it all out

Except when he taught.
Clear when he fought –
for the vulnerable
oppressed,
against racist
pub landlords.
Or fascist fucks

Killed by police.
Beaten in Southall
they caved in his skull
couldn't get up
or hold a glass.
Died in a Hospital theatre.
11.40pm, 23 April, 1979

Waiting Room

Four Walls
Harsh Lights
Blue carpet
Flip chart
Bottled water
Boiled sweets
Black coffee
Biscuits
Awaiting others
Deliberations
No sense of time
Muffled voices
Closed Doors
Deja Vu
Have they forgotten me?
Case law
Documents
Evidence
Me in a suit?
The Accused
Franz Kafka's
The Trial
Tribulations
Mitigations
Impossible situations
Insight
Outside
Remote
Remorse
Recourse
Witness statement
Cross examine
Perjury
Contaminated
Implicated
Abrogated

Innocent
Inside
Who lied?
Smoking gun......

wallet

I wish I could find
a wallet
on the floor.
Just like ones
I found before –
my back
is up against
a wall.

I look for coins
on pavements,
in the gutter.
I see fag-butts
at the fag end
of the day.

Too desperate to
look up at the sky,
I remember
when I used to smoke,
I'd pick them up,
make a
match thin
Borstal cigarette.

Now I look
for wallets
along the
passenger side
of parked cars
because my need
is greater than
all yours.

I wish I'd thought
like this
a week ago –
when I found
one abandoned
near a pub.
Instead I turn,
meekly hand it in.

Now I walk
past that pub
in case misfortune –
like lightning –
strikes again,
and lightens
my load.
Now I have
more mouths to
feed.

A landlord shout –
stops me in my tracks!
Beckons me inside
I'm taken aback!

Here within –
a place I can't afford.
Then he says
the magic word, "Reward!".

A wad of –
rolled up £5 notes,
and it brings
a lump into my throat

Lifts up
the dark clouds of my mood,
and I hurry
home! With drink and food....

Recovery

Listen therapist – we need to talk. There are things you don't see with your brief therapy and half a dozen sessions before you set me free. With your emphasis on illness and diagnosis; hoarding symptoms like stamp collectors after an illusive Penny Black. You medicalize social problems as our fault, but we cannot be wished away. Are we ill because we're depressed or is it because we're oppressed? And is the key to this oppression being robbed of self expression?

There's a riot in my head – but just like Martin Luther King said, "Riots are conversations of the voiceless". And 'we' lost our voice because 'you' usurped our language. Let's take the term 'recovery'. For health professionals like you it becomes an excuse to cease treatment, eliminate resources; deny us the 'luxury' of difference. In your hands, the Langue has no Parole*

But 'we' invented the term 'recovery' as a way to understand our difficulties. It's how we hold onto the past and recover identity. It stops us being written off. Just as Lord Byron said,"Deformity is daring...", and we strive to make good, catch up and maybe overtake those who have not felt the pain of emotional overload. And as we re-calibrate our pain we echo Kurt Cobain when he wrote, "Thank you for the tragedy. I need it for my art"

*Barthes, R. (1972). *Mythologies*

The Blast
Written on the 10th anniversary of the 7/7 bombings

If you hadn't made me late that morning, I would have caught the train on time. You, just a small child in need of comfort: I, a parent who couldn't resist a hug. So anyway, I caught the later train. That journey known to all – Bristol Parkway, Swindon, Didcot, Reading and London Paddington. From there onto Kings Cross or Euston. It wasn't until way past Swindon, we knew something was wrong

First one to crack was the driver - garbled message said he couldn't go on. Journey would end at the next station. Heard him sob like a small child over the Tannoy. The news spread along each carriage – a 'Mexican wave' of terror via mobile phone. We scramble for news second hand. Piece together a picture of Kings Cross afire. Rumours of bombs elsewhere – everywhere!

Driver gets bullied by the fat controller. He'll drive on to Reading - fresh driver there. We can start making plans. Someone's phone goes off – the ringtone is, "Should I Stay Or Should I Go?" Another 9/11? I rush to the toilets to record a defiant goodbye message. Voice breaks towards the end – I wonder how come the Americans are better at doing this stuff? Is it because of all the John Wayne movies they watch? Sod it – next time I'll just send a text. My wife will wonder why Stephen Hawking is pledging his undying love...

Finally, onto Paddington – conference cancelled today. I phone people to keep them away. My pregnant wife phones and we argue. She wants me to come home – I utter the fatal words, "But we can't give in to terror – if I come home they've won". Like they won't plant bombs coz I'm here. That'll scare 'em. *I've* watched too many John Wayne movies… Paddington begins to stifle. Elsewhere a worried wife has a miscarriage. I go for a walk - a bus goes "bang!"

Blood red dead – the smell of the blood! mixing with the cordite. 'Fight or flight' mechanism – head says "run", heart says "stay". As days go by new rituals are created. Lamp post posters of missing and dead left by relatives – like posters for missing pets. And the peace and unity vigils, where we learnt terror was indiscriminate – kills all faiths. Just like the bombs on Baghdad – war is terror

I was lucky – didn't die.... But carry the dead with me every night – I see their blackened disfigured faces crowding out my mind, and they sound like 'James and the Giant Peach' when they say, "Where were you – we were waiting for you?" And the menacing Blood Red Dead drops into my head – says, "I took your place – so why weren't you there on time? This should have been you not me..."

And I can't take this anymore....
And I just....can't....take....this....anymore......
And I am the resurrection.....

Barmpot

I'm a little barmpot, short and stout.
People back away from me when I begin to shout.

It's not at them I'm shouting – I'm responding to the din
created by demons that dwell within.

They compete with different voices, giving me hell.
I drown them with headphones, but I'm under their spell.

I'm told they're parts of my shattered personality –
But how can shards of self show hatred towards me?

I've been shoved on a locked ward to 'protect me from harm'.
But the staff just ignore me when I sound alarmed.

The nurses look like school kids who stole my pocket money,
and bullied me till I ran and cried to mummy.

But home was where the voices were – interrogating me.
Then the voices all took shape as things I could see.

Doctors tried drugs – I 'pill rolled' like a jerk.
It's clear to any idiot that drugs don't fucking work.

They've finally decided I can have art therapy,
I'll draw the bloody demons so they all at last can see.

They've given me some pencils, left me free to draw,
faces of the demons – ones that I abhor.

My food tastes like it's poison, from meals I shall withdraw.
My skin feels clothed with insects – I feel them crawl and claw.

I've sharpened up a pencil, shoved it through my eye.
I can't cope with this torture – so its time to die.

I'm a little barmpot, all snuffed out.
Put me in a bodybag and carry me out.

[24]

Would That I'd Died That Night

I was the girl
The one with Pompe's Disease –
a neuro-muscular disorder
I became
a constellation of symptoms
I was the disease –
a disability
Robbed of all personhood
They told me I'd be dead by 21
So I tried to kill myself at 17
As I clambered over the side of the bridge
a voice in my head told me to stop
Or maybe it was just cowardice
whistling through the wind and icy cold
Either way, had I jumped
I would have missed out on the last 45 years –
going to University, motherhood,
becoming a grandmother
I know I have defied the odds –
have I not the right to be defiant?
Now the chattering classes –
'Guardian' readers and the like –
want to give me the 'right' to die
'Assisted Suicide' they call it
Does this mean a disabled life is worth less?
(worthless!)
In which case beware –
as prejudice comes dressed up as 'rights'

II.

'The poet who is making a political statement and is dealing with a social situation – who is writing from the people to the people – must perforce use the language of the people, not the private rarified language of the poet.'
Linton Kwesi Johnson

Nicotine

Sit looking stunned
Nothing else left
The taste on your tongue
The smell on your breath

Stains on your fingers
Holes in your toes
Stale smells that linger
Stud in your nose

It goes with the leather
And faded ripped jeans
But it's hard to tell whether
You've come apart at the seams

Cancer's your star sign
As well as your fate
A haze in the sunshine
That's how you relate

To the glow in an ashtray
Which lights up your face
Where dead matches at last lay
And a drag sets the pace

Like a clock that is ticking
Away at life's measure
And the ash that you're flicking
Is like discarded treasure

From a burnt out old ruin
That once was a home
As you sit there smoking
Cigarettes on your own

The Blue Mug

I use the blue mug
because I...
like the colour?
I put the
kettle on,
I look up
through the
glass ceiling.
See the clouds
moving back and
forth – colliding
and separating.
Isn't it amazing
how they do this?
I could watch all day...

I use the blue mug –
but the kettle's
boiled dry.
A room full of steam –
but it's not steam,
It's fog.
I'm lost in
the fog, and
only small. I'm
scared and
call for my dad
you are there
and you
hold my hand.
I don't know who you are...

I use the blue mug
because it's
blue for a boy and,
"I'm a boy, I'm a boy –
but if I say I am I get it!" *
I can remember
song lyrics
from 50 years ago
but I can't answer
the visitor's questions.
They ask
what year it is
who the
Prime Minister is,
and about arithmetic.
I tell them I'm
no good at this.
They should ask
my brother Glyn.
Done his eleven plus.
Knows his pounds,
shillings and pence.

I use the blue mug
so that I know
which one
is mine.
You stand there,
say you are
my wife.
But you
can't be.
You are
an old lady,
and I
am only young.

I want to
run away –
but my legs
don't work properly.
I think you are
a witch – and
you cast a
spell on them.
I shout and
scream at
you to let
me go.
If only
mum & dad
could see me...

I use...
the blue
mug because...
I can't
fucking
remember
anything.
There was
something about
blue and the
'Blue Danube'
is a piece
of music
and there's
blue in
the sky
and there was
something about
a girl
and the

Prime Minister
and a mug –
a cup
of coffee?
And there's
20 shillings to
the pound
and I don't
know where
I am.
I don't
know what
I'm doing,
and I'm scared.
For God's sake –
Can't somebody
help me?

* 'I'm a Boy' - *The Who*

Another Day

If I seem too slow
It's because I'm not the human dynamo
You used to know

If I start to cry
It's because I can't believe the lie
That's just passed me by

If I seem too free
It's because of what used to be
In the past has meant to me

If I appear down
And sorrow starts to drown
Don't worry – I'll turn around

If I seem all through
Before I look at you
It's what I used to do

If I cannot stay
Before I melt away
I'll be in yesterday

Before you become bound
The future which is found
You'll hear without a sound

Turn over new leaf
Challenge old belief
Feel the relief

Falling from the top
Just like the watch you'll stop
See the body drop

I Am Dying

Give me a pauper's grave
no-one to pray / soul to save

No crucifix or obelisk
Where dogs stop and piss

None to stop and cry
where bones lie

No mourning relatives
no last 'Will' to give

Nothing but debts
past regrets

No longer want to live
no more to give

Except to count
each breath wrung out

Millions of memories
erased in frame freeze

Give me a pauper's grave –
a life fettered like a slave

Sisyphus rolls stone uphill
life's labours kill

Funeral Etiquette

Never have sex at a funeral, if you do –
don't have sex with the corpse.
Relatives don't like it. This one's a cremation.
Don't wear loose fitting clothing or bracelets –
in case you get hooked to the casket
Dragged to the furnace –
where flesh smells like burning pork.

Never laugh at a funeral – even when they play 'Abide With Me'
by Harry Secombe on vinyl, and the record gets stuck:
'Me-click! Me-click! Me-click! Me-click! Me-click!'
Resist the urge to sing 'a name I call myself'
in a bizarre 'Abide With Me/Do-Re-Mi' mash up.
Stifle that laugh – banish thoughts of Harry Secombe
as 'Neddie Seagoon' on the Goon Show.
Do not start humming the 'Ying Tong Song' – hold it in.

Never ask strangers who they are related to on a day like this.
If half the people stood outside look like total strangers,
it's because they are lost in the mist – looking at the wrong flowers.
They look confused – mutter a strangers name under their breath.
Bewildered – they avoid attracting attention and make
non-committal small talk before fading out of sight.

Never get talked into looking after uncle John – the poor old git is
dementing. He can no longer tell the difference between weddings,
funerals and christenings. Honour bound to enact his usual party
    piece,
he'll put his false teeth into someone else's drink, get up, propose a
toast, make a speech and half way through, drop his trousers.

Never spend too much time with the old ladies – with faces like
    gargoyles,
they have razor sharp memories and will recount every embarrassing

moment of your misspent childhood – whilst cackling like witches.
Avoid the in-laws/cousins/siblings – mainly 'outlaws'. They'll
happily recall how they broke each others arms in fights and how
they used to pick you up and flush your head down the toilet.

In fact –
never, never, never go to funerals at all...
Just send your condolences.

Ironing Doesn't Do Itself You Know

After 3 cups of coffee I am ready
to face the ordeal of 'Downstairsworld',
a place of many challenges –
worst of which is the 'Spittingsnarlingiron'.

'Spittingsnarlingiron' should live in a cupboard
but can often be found glaring at me from
a back room with one orange eye.
It often contemptuously blows steam out of its nostrils –
not unlike a Dragon with small man syndrome.

This beast drinks plenty of water.
Other horrors await in 'Downstairsworld' –
if not careful they will distract you
and 'Spittingsnarlingiron' will strike like a venomous snake.

There are 2 tribes for a start off.
One is called the 'Haveyouseenee' – I think they fought the Romans.
They ask a lot of questions, like "Have you seen the Pritt Stick?" or
"Have you seen my coat?"

The other tribe are the 'Wouldja'.
I am surprised they never perished like the Picts
as they seem almost completely useless, and ask questions like
"Wouldja iron my T-shirt?" or "Wouldja iron this skirt?"

Whilst distracted the 'Spittingsnarlingiron' struck –
I sank its red hot fangs into my left hand,
just as I was trying to put a 'Crease' into a collar.
A 'Crease' is a small cat-like creature – they don't like collars...

I immediately fled into the kitchen to run cold water over my wound
where I was accosted by a young member of the 'Haveyouseenee'
    tribe
He said, "I can't believe it – when you put washing in the machine it's
all crumpled, but when it comes out the other end it's neatly folded....
It's like magic!"

The Girl Who Jumped When Things Went Bang

She hated it when doors slammed or
things went bang on Bonfire Night.

She had a crazy father with fire
in his eyes, who beat her mother
and any other child within
the house, except her brother –

who, instructed in the art
of Misogyny, went on to
beat his wife too.

But the girl who jumped when things went bang
grew into a woman –
who could fly into inexplicable rage one minute,
and cuddle a baby off to sleep the next.

She still retained her fear of the dark –
of storms, of sudden change.

It had been the same ever since,
as a child, she found a severed
arm after the bombing raid.
It was 1942.

A Child's Purgatory In Wales

Me and my friend Sean
engaged in our favourite game –
'Waiting for the daddies'
We – toddlers both
awaiting men who looked like giants
Donkey jacketed – back from the steelworks
they would lift us and throw us up into the sky
and plonk us on their shoulders
Sometimes my dad would hug me first
and stubble would dig into my neck –
It tickled!
And there was a sweetness on his breath –
bacardi and coke

And then home – to a mam who cooked
Later there would be stories, games and music
with brothers and sisters
before going to bed – carried over dad's shoulders –
to a cot in the corner of my parents bedroom
Morning brought its own uncertainties
Was the bed wet or dry?
A dry day was a good day
and mam was sweetness and light
I would call her from the cot,
get carried downstairs for breakfast
and play in a garden of apple trees and roses –
tinted like my specs

Wet days were dark and stormy – like the weather
The room more grey
and I was too nervous to call
She was the judge you'd dread
as she stormed across the room
with a 'Thwack!' on the head
or slap across the legs

"I'll make you dance" she said –
like a baddie in a 'spaghetti western'
Or "Shall I rub your nose in it?",
which was how we punished the dog...

That was an age ago...
Nothing remains of then
except a nervous inner-child
and a rocking horse,
which still stares at me accusingly
from a corner of the attic

Abuse Of Power

Why do you carry on as normal?
Respectable life – everything formal

After what you did to me,
recurring nightmares – can't break free

What did I do to deserve your attention?
'Special' games too sick to mention

Are you so blind you cannot see
damage you did – emotionally?

You never once apologized
now all affection is despised

My body just an empty shell
going through a private hell

Breaking down the wall of trust
to satisfy a teenage thrust

All your weaknesses restyled
take advantage of younger child

To sample things you couldn't get
– in later life I can't forget

I learned to hate the way you loved
The iron fist : the velvet glove

The world collapsed in yesterday
I never grew or learnt to play

I hid myself away instead
and wished that I could wake up dead

The tears still flow from an age ago
What I did wrong I still don't know

I wasn't ready for sexual pleasure
to be abused at your leisure

Skeletons in cupboards try to hide –
It's me that's bloody crucified

They say that blood is thicker than water
Mine congealed in innocence slaughter

How come you came out on top?
Whilst my self torture doesn't stop

I cry myself to sleep at night
and give up on all future fight

Your life goes on without a hitch
My nerves have gone – I stammer and twitch

I withdrew from old nature's game
and drink a lot to keep myself sane

If I were to 'copycat' my abuse
would this explanation be much use?

How come I paid for your insecurity
with the money and the fags you threw as a lure at me?

Incest is a dirty word
A crime unseen a crime unheard

Des-olation

'Stars' pour out of coffee cups
onto my table
and drip into chairs next to me –
caffeine infected
They talk incessantly
about themselves –
their plans / dreams / schemes / affectations –
They're style obsessed
Obsessed with the look of desolation /
things that fall apart / of built-in obsolescence
They mistake me for a kindred spirit
I am merely fuelled on spirits
Meaner than a mere caffeiner
I'm the scion of real self neglect
A carelessness in my demeanor
which goes beyond
ratter-tatteredness
of trendy hipstered-fashionistas
I really choke on my own vomit
I'm the unseen gatecrasher at every party –
last 'guest' to leave
One still drinking the morning after
No hangovers for me....
No pain killers with my coffee
I imbibe my passion like my vodka – neat!
The one-night-stand
that makes breakfast in your kitchen
while you're seeing double
and still bitchin'...
about your hangover from the night before
I won't leave my telephone number
this was just a place for slumber –
you were only slumming it anyway....
I have a greater – more self destructive – hunger....
to race towards the end of days.

Heads and Hearts

I will prove
my strength
by cutting
off my
feelings.
No connection, no
attunement, no trust.
I shall
decapitate
my head,
rip out
my heart,
shave off
my skin,
snip away
my tongue,
neutralise
each nerve,
pull out
my eyes,
remove
my gut,
amputate
my legs
and feet –
so I cannot
walk in
the other
person's shoes,
strip off
each sinew
down to the
bare bones,
keep cutting and
slashing, screaming
"Sacrifice! Sacrifice!",

until there's
nothing left.
Then I
shall become a
selfish
bastard
just like you....

Is Not A Home....

What do you do
when the magic fades
a house
not really ours
elaborate hoax
monopoly money
ethereal
not realizeable cash
nothing you can spend
maybe one day
it will be ripped away
to pay the bill
where you lie in bed
no investment
for the children
until then we decorate
we paint the walls with arguments
there's blood red anger doors
we wallpaper the dining room
with laughter, happiness
and warmth
the pattern fades with time
damp in the walls
paper comes away
revealing crumbling plaster
broken brickwork
silverfish
at least the photos remain
happier times
when all was possible
we seemed
immortal –
not tired
now
we look like ghosts

outgrowth

I do not need you –
cause of arguments
guess and second guess
attempt to mind read
fill in gaps
cannot reach you
feel the friction

You do not need me –
have a dog
mindless barking
preferential treatment
pets come first

My grandfathers
were Black
and Irish
further down
the food chain

Their wives didn't
need them either
had dogs
of their own
Why bark yourself?

Homeless

It's the things you lose
moving from one house to another
Another night – another sofa
Man in the DWP
tells me not to say I'm homeless
"Get a 'care of' address," he says
"then you'll only have to sign on once a fortnight"
'Care of' address gets sick of me being around
Funny things parents
So it's sofa surfing
Sometimes sleeping on someone's floor
I have a sleeping bag
and rucksack
But it is the things....
that you lose –
My 'TRB' CD
no 'Power in the Darkness'....
And Court papers
I wonder if I'll ever
live with my wife and kids again
Or....is it over?
Hunger kicks in –
the 'God Squad' provide breakfast
Jesus doesn't want me for a sunbeam
but his disciples make a mean black coffee
Free internet at the Library –
it keeps you out of the cold
I am my own agent again –
I go to see a film
catch up with some old friends,
read books and listen to music
get put on the 'guest list' at gigs
take my kid to football
Stay over at weekends....
then my wife decides
she wants me to come back

paws for thought

When people ask,
"What's wrong?",
I can bat them away
with the phrase –
"Black Dog stuff".

Then I don't
have to explain
nausea –
morning sickness
of the mind.

Or my
perfectionist heart –
shredding thoughts,
actions, utterances;
a form of
deliberate self-harm.

Eventually my
Freudian slip mind
bites back –
you are no longer
scary, all
powerful – I
am no longer
in your grasp.

You are now
a child's toy –
just a
"stuffed black dog".
I can put you
back in the box.

III.

'I have – I know it, I feel it – set my foot on a soil of freedom where nothing hinders the soaring of human thought. It would be an insult to you not to open to you my whole soul and my whole heart.'
Anatole France

On the buses…

A single ticket to Newport:
is all I bloody need
A single ticket to Newport:
with small change I plead
A single ticket to Newport:
I've got kids to feed
A single ticket to Newport:
get flirty and I'll breed
A single ticket to Newport:
hair that does recede
A single ticket to Newport:
cut me and I'll bleed
A single ticket to Newport:
aggression fuelled by speed
A single ticket to Newport:
addiction is the creed
A single ticket to Newport:
anxiety is freed
A single ticket to Newport:
I'll follow any lead
A single ticket to Newport:
challenge me - I'll cede

A single ticket to Newport:
aw – c'mon fuckin' driver
A single ticket to Newport:
wot – no change from a fiver?
A single ticket to Newport:
feel breath mixed with saliva
A single ticket to Newport:
I ain't no duck'n'diver....
A single ticket to Newport.
Look mate – I'm a survivor......

That's Life

Life is shit
then you die
Ask the question
Wonder why
Here's blood and betrayal
in your eye
God is for sale
with pie in the sky
When love's in your vein
predictable high
Look in the mirror
reflection's a lie
Kiss the girls
watch them fly
Pick yourself up
Well, you've got to try
Dust yourself down
Start to cry
Dealing despair
An endless supply
No escape from this pain
No 'right of reply'
Why so polite to my face
when you can't deny
you put the knife in my back
but hate being told that you're sly?
So look at the freak
and then decry
Just remember the make up
on which you rely
hides an insecure being
as imperfect as I

Stoned

I'm like a pebble on a beach
with shingle running over me –
A scraping of ecstasy
with the passing of the tides
which are over too soon
I am left alone again
with the sun beating down on me
Bleaching me white
and baking the residue of salt
Until I crack –
at least inside I feel I do
But this is never really true
Appetite's whetted by the sea in you
In reality
you were a piece of shingle
which was soon past
Only myself, the sun and sand
are still here
The skimming stone of life goes on

The Remote Console

Sometimes I look at you
and think –
just dreaming really....
Then I listen
and start to sink
When you pour out your troubles
I want to drink your heart
But that's kept away
with the silverware
and crockery
For special occasions
and special people
Not me....
I'm the invisible man

in your estimation
I'm real and I'm
here and I care
When things are fine
you run straight past me
to greet a lover
When things fall apart –
there is no other
You can find me
Tired and alone...
The remote console

You're never alone with a loan

I wish I won the lottery
I haven't done it yet
Only way I've got to be
free of loans and debt

Electric meter has a key
TV licence a card
I top things up gingerly –
budgeting is hard

Debts I can't pay get set aside
against my bloody home
Can't pay the mortgage – though I've tried
I'm in the danger zone

The interest keeps growing
on various debts I owe
Bastards keep on moaning
I confront bailiffs toe-to-toe

They charge me for letters
they keep sending in the post
Printing money without fetters –
moving up my debt goalposts

Ran out of cash completely
Got a loan before payday
They dealt with it curtly –
payday's turned to 'mayday'

There's no longer any slack
to carry out repairs
Home looks like a dosser's shack
I slip into despair

I find it difficult to sleep
I creep around the house
Door knock, or the phone goes 'bleep!' –
I'm quiet as a mouse

I'm supposed to be the breadwinner
Supposed to pay the bills
These are the thoughts that linger
They wear me down – it kills

Should I try to front it out
or file for bankruptcy?
I can't seem to turn shit around
The bastards 'own' a part of me

I'd like to post the fucking key
back through my own front door
Disappear eternally –
not look back no more

Missing Payment

There is no money
no amount
has turned up
in my bank account
so I dial the number
wait in the queue
for about
an hour or two –
then you say 'bear with me....'

I get wound up
you start to flounder –
do you believe the myths
about benefit scroungers?
Look – if you don't
restore my payments
I will end up
on the pavement –
and you say 'bear with me....'

I bet you've got
a landlord too
who wants to be paid
on time from you
we're all being shafted
tell the truth
all we need's
a bloody roof –
and you say 'bear with me....'

Bear with me? Bear with me?
There's a fucking Bear with me
There's an Elephant in the room
By a big black dog I'm being consumed
No amount of breathin' in a paper bag
can stop a full on panic attack –
so don't just say 'bear with me....'

[59]

What's love got to do with it?

You can walk down that street
approach a group of girls
with frost bitten white-white legs
poking out from micro-mini skirts
You can satisfy every kink and desire –
for the right price –

You can be whipped, beaten stamped on
with pointy high stiletto heels
She'll walk up and down your body
whilst you cry out in pain and ecstasy
You can dress up like a baby
and get spanked when you urinate

You can ignore the pimp inspired
pin-cushion needle marks on some arms
and tell yourself
everybody pays for sex right?
Even married men –
what do you think a mortgage is?
And these girls are there for the excitement –
glamour in otherwise dull lives
The glamour and romance
of exchanging cash and bodily fluids

You can walk away again too
once you've satisfied desires
There are other things you don't see
You miss the graffiti
Not the arty ghetto spray paint variety
Not postcode gangland mark your territory
'Westside boyz' style
It's not cheeky sub-Banksy anti capitalist
'eat the rich' stylised ironic humour
It's written in Biro by frozen shaky hands
on walls and in doorways
where those girls hang out
It simply says, 'We're doing this to feed our kids'...

Abandon

I run down the hill as dawn breaks
A slippery slope in mist and rain
Get to the bus stop –
journey to work
Funny how I've committed to memory
exactly how late the bus will be
Extract the fare to ride
As I near my destination
I notice a Pigeon sitting on a telephone cable
Only, it looks like a Buzzard or Vulture
or sort of bird that follows starving children around
waiting for them to die in an African famine....
And work is 'care work' – devalued and privatised
Minimum wage slavery
Bosses who look like a modern take on a Dickens novel
'Hard Times' indeed – the new Gradgrinds
with pound sign eyes
Each new resident is nothing more
than part of the down payment on the next Porsche
As I approach the old 'living' bone factory
I swear I see the company logo
change into a picture of the horned beast
The name beneath
transforms into words –
'Abandon self respect all ye who enter here...'

Workmates

Late and never early
Short, fat and curly
Big strong and burly
Lots of bleached hair and fake tanned girlies
Some are Romanian
another Hungarian
one says she's Sagittarian
And I think one's a vegetarian
One of them just got the sack –
workmates stabbed him in the back
Left him to take all the flack
You've got to have a real thick skin
keep your head down to fit in
We count the minutes until break
where we can make our brief escape
let off steam and just piss-take
We share each other's sandwiches
across half a dozen languages
Find that we can feel at ease
beyond borders and boundaries
But then – 'oh no, here comes the boss'
I couldn't really give a toss
Because me – well, I've got a big gob
Tell him I think he's a knob
It's time I found a new job

Cladding

Reflective –
going nowhere.
Legs that have
failed. Knows
it's the end.
Calls his son
to say goodbye.
Tells him how
he would dance –
busting shapes
inside his mother's
belly – to Michael
Jackson in shops.
Beautiful boy –
he slept well
in his cot.

Moves towards closure –
to say, "I love you".
Gets distracted by
bubbling heat.
Stirring thoughts of,
when much younger,
he worked in a fast food store.
Saw a spider trapped
on a hamburger island,
in an industrial broiler.
It exploded in the heat.
It shouldn't end like this.
Just charcoal now…

Aberfan Man

He was unmistakable
A lecturer you'd dread
Old school –
did not give handouts
Would dictate notes
in front of a lecture theatre –
'tut' if you didn't keep up
Yet he got us through
that most difficult of subjects –
Anatomy and Physiology
Remember how he used to
describe mitochondria as
looking like upside-down woodlice?
He didn't mix well or exchange small talk
He had a red bulbous nose, white hair
and hip flask full of whiskey
Spare bottles kept in cupboards
so he would never run out
You could smell the whiskey in his sweat
or on his breath sometimes
It had been this way
since as a young medic
he had driven past Aberfan
When all things bright and beautiful
were crushed beneath the spoil
Buried alive by the National Coal Board
He spent days there – uncountable hours
Digging with bare hands at first
to get the bodies out.....
He never went back
Never had closure
Never visited the memorial stone
Which read –
Dedicated to 116 children and 28 adults
Who lost their lives October 21st 1966
To those we love
And miss so very much.

Lieberries

The 'Lieberry' – a plant which started off infesting gardens
They look like Wild Lilies but are in fact poisonous weeds
Their aroma has infected the human psyche:
a pungent smell transforms chlorophyl into chloroform,
which numbs the brain – replacing good sense with common sense
An appeal to the lowest common denominator
Early indications include repetition of the phrase,
'There is no alternative'
Once ideation takes hold, sufferers in positions of power
attempt to destroy all that we hold in common by decimating public
    services
Justifying this with talk of 'market forces' and statements such as –
'Library cuts are getting disproportionate attention because they are a
"middle class" issue'*
'Changes are needed to library services because the council has
committed to cut £1.1m from its annual budget' **
'We now need to make £117m of savings next year, rising to £338m by
2017/18.This is on top of the £462m we have had to save so far.' ***

The only solution....
is to cut every Lieberry branch one by one
Dig them up at the roots
Eradicate every one –
then get rid of all the lying liars who are too far gone –
intoxicated by this noxious poison
Or stop them enunciating such pernicious nonsense
In their fog of Lieberry fumes....

* www.morningstaronline.co.uk/a-2e79-Manics-singer-boosts-library-campaign
** www.bbc.co.uk/news/uk-england-bristol-31592889
*** www.theguardian.com/uk-news/2014/dec/10/birmingham-city-council-axe-thousands-jobs-cuts

Ta Ta Tan Toc?

My daddy was a steelworker
he worked at "Castle Works"
Callaghan betrayed Cardiff
it's the last time that he worked

Then my older brother
he worked at GKN
Thatcher and MacGregor
attacked steelworkers again

Then the 'gruesome twosome'
turned their minds to coal
consigning miners' communities
to poverty on the dole

Now their market madness
stripped bare for all to see
a pack of business locusts
call time on industry

The gruesome twosome's lovechild
sat in number ten
watching as the steelworkers
paid the price again

Robbing cash from poor to rich
David Cameron
was a modern day
Sheriff of Nottingham

He bought cheap steel from China
while ours paid China's tariffs
all with the agreement of
China's favourite sheriff...

Tata's vultures will come for plant
They'll come to asset strip
occupy the steelworks
Don't let them take one bit

The future of Port Talbot
I'm sure you realize
could be like pit villages
we need to organise

This Government's mean-but-weak
Let's force open their eyes
we are the majority
when we shout, *Nationalise!*

We Fought The Law Back

The Poll Tax Riot was a lot of fun –
we fought the law back – and we won
The Poll Tax Riot was a lot of fun
we fought the law back – and we won

A big fat pig came on the 'News at Ten' –
said, "I think we lost it a bit"
I taped it on a video so I could see again
Thatcher's boot boys turn to shit

The cops wanted a riot and they got one –
we fought the law back – and we won
The cops wanted a riot and they got one
we fought the law back – and we won

Someone shouted "burn South Africa House"
Apartheid's bunker's already on fire
pissed off crowds make the cops retreat –
resistance flames grow higher and higher

And there's no future – for Thatcher!
There's no future – in England's green and....
It's time to wake up!

The ghost of Frida Kahlo

Did you see her
at the conference?
She throttled
Theresa May.

Being worn,
an appendage
on that clammy wrist,
an affront to
Frida's bisexuality,
disability,
blood red Communism.

Poltergeist Frida
ripped words off walls
the way she tore
through life;
with eyes like fire.

Elsewhere –
'Diego Rivera Reloaded',
painted a new mural
with a P45 on,
and a laughing Frida Kahlo –
wearing a
'Theresa May' bracelet.
Who the hell
needs Banksy anyway?

To a Lib-Dem Candidate

Knock on the door for my vote
I'll shake you warmly – by the throat

You're about as child-friendly as the late Cyril Smith –
sex scandals and cover-ups, ain't there a whiff?

Mike Hancock, Mark Oaten and Lord Rennard
and Paddy – is keeping your pants on so hard?

Now you're in bed with Changeling Chuka –
has to be said – unprincipled fucker

Is it bullshit I'm smelling or hypocrisy?
I remember you said you'd scrap tuition fees…

You all live on a yellow submarine
sink without trace – nowhere to be seen

Except the odd enclave where you may hold out
Where voters are gluttons for punishment no doubt

What's that daft bird symbol supposed to be?
Looks more like an Albatross than a Phoenix to me

Next time use a Dodo or something extinct
maybe voters might just see the link

I don't mean to taunt you – don't mean to be mean:
you all live in a yellow glum machine

I met a candidate – seemed a nice chap
I told him I thought the Lib-Dems were crap

"We'll still be king makers in Parliament", he said –
the place that gained power chopping off a king's head?

He said a hung Parliament – that was his hope.
I want a hung Parliament too – done with rope!

That's not where the power to change things resides –
it's in the streets and the protests outside....

You Never Arrived
The ghosts of Calais

Avoid the trap
Of vengeance –
Turning on us
When Terrorists massacre kids
We ran away from men who plant bombs,
Wield guns – demand absolute power –
Our enemies too
Why we are here
If I had not left Syria I would have died
If I stay in "the jungle" over winter I could die too
In a donated tent
Easy tinder for a tarpaulin Kristallnacht
Bonfires of hatred
We came to Europe to find the land of human rights
Instead we are left here in this camp
Even asylum seekers
If we could get a proper roof we would stay
No solution
Here in this hell hole
We must escape from this place
Higher fences / more cops
Make it harder to leave
Borders are too strong
Death returns –
A Syrian run over on the motorway
In front of her son,
An Afghan boy hit by a train
I join the protests on the roundabout –
'Open the borders!'
My friend lives in hope
He'll make it to Britain
Has relatives there
Others pray for salvation
I will no longer pray for myself.....

I've seen pictures in newspapers visitors bring –
Dead babies washed up on the shore
I fall on my knees
Prostrate myself
Pray for those who never arrived…

Shoes

Babies shoes never worn
Left by a mother
for her daughter
in the rubble in Raqqa
Where there used to be a school
till some bloody minded fool
decided to bomb Syria

It was the only epitaph
for her dead and pregnant daughter
No time to mourn between the slaughter
which is being inflicted on us
who have done nothing
by those who have done everything
but admit nothing

A thousand maniacs inhabit our world
Some wear uniforms
Some some wear suits
Some wear black
But none of them mourn
They want to pile up the dead
like chips in a casino

My Last Journey

'Two feet of a victim whose body vanished in a single puff;
they stood upright, stuck to the concrete road'
– *Kenzaburo Oe*, Hiroshima Notes

Two feet
Tall
Erect
They stand there
awaiting
the return of my body
Where am I?
Did I really breathe
in the white heat?
Was I blinded
by light
as the radiation
ripped through me?
Did I get the chance
to cry out in pain?
Beg mercy for my
mother, father, sister,
brother, lover, daughter?
Or did I just vaporize?
Disappear
into the ether?
Were these
my last thoughts?
Or the imaginings
of another –
looking at
remains
at the epicentre:
Hiroshima?

Sleep

I should go to bed
before it gets light
but there are things
which bother me at night

One of them is hunger –
we are short of food
nothing in the cupboard
to feed a growing brood

Another is affection,
like *Love's Labour's Lost*
every spurned tenderness –
rejection has a cost

Then there is my skin
how it bloody thickens
with each blow and insult –
deep inside it sickens

There's a different hunger –
we need to re-arrange
the world that we subsist in
I'm hungry for the change

Another affection
wells inside of me
against bigotry and hatred
for humanity

Sickness is systemic
or so it seems to me,
I'll off, away to bed,
dreams can set you free

[76]